Guess What

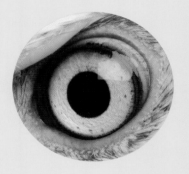

CHERRY
LAKE
Publishing

Published in the United States of America by
Cherry Lake Publishing
Ann Arbor, Michigan
www.cherrylakepublishing.com

Content Adviser: Susan Heinrichs Gray
Reading Adviser: Marla Conn, ReadAbility, Inc.
Book Design: Felicia Macheske

Photo Credits: © FloridaStock/Shutterstock.com, cover; © Eric Isselée/Shutterstock.com, 1, 4, 14, back cover;
© Martin Dallaire/Shutterstock.com, 3, 8 ; © Sergey Uryadnikov/Shutterstock.com, 7, 21; © Teri Virbickis/Shutterstock.com, 11;
© Steve Byland/Shutterstock.com, 13; © Nancy Bauer/Shutterstock.com, 16; © predrag1/Thinkstock, 19;
© Andrey_Kuzmin/Shutterstock.com, back cover

Library of Congress Cataloging-in-Publication Data

Calhoun, Kelly, author.
 Feathered and fierce / Kelly Calhoun.
 pages cm. — (Guess what)
 Summary: "Young children are natural problem solvers and always looking for answers, especially when it involves animals.
Guess What: Feathered and Fierce: Bald Eagle provides young curious readers with striking visual clues and simply written hints.
Using the photos and text, readers rely on visual literacy skills, reading, and reasoning as they solve the animal mystery. Clearly
written facts give readers a deeper understanding of how the animal lives. Additional text features, including a glossary and an
index, help students locate information and learn new words."— Provided by publisher.
 Audience: Ages 5-8.
 Audience: K to grade 3.
 ISBN 978-1-63362-624-9 (hardcover) — ISBN 978-1-63362-714-7 (pbk.) — ISBN 978-1-63362-804-5 (pdf)
— ISBN 978-1-63362-894-6 (ebook)
 1. Bald eagle—Juvenile literature. [1. Eagles.] I. Title.

QL696.F32C34 2016
598.9'42—dc23

2015003119

Cherry Lake Publishing would like to acknowledge the work of The Partnership for 21st Century Skills.
Please visit *www.p21.org* for more information.

Printed in the United States of America
Corporate Graphics Inc.

Table of Contents

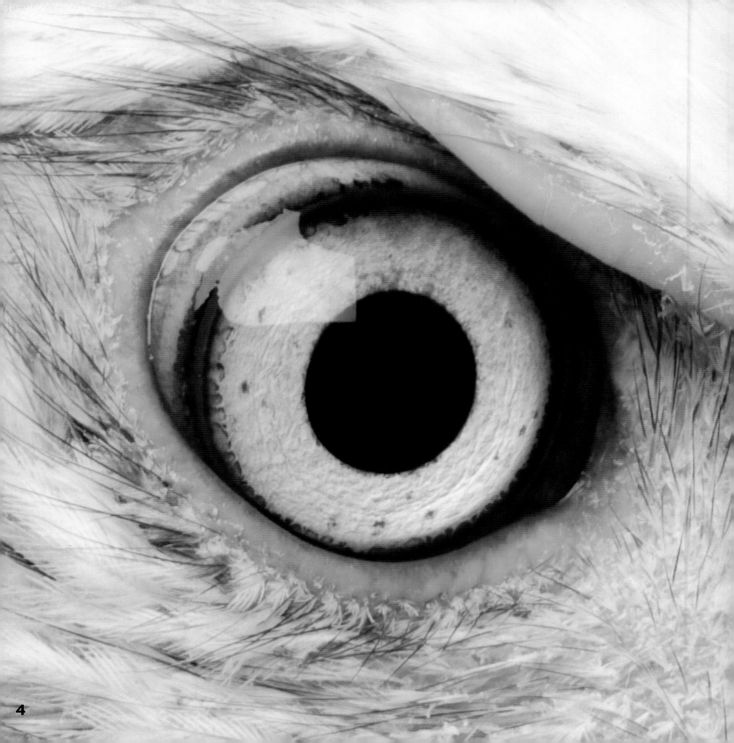

My eyes see very well.

I fly with
my strong
wings.

My body is covered with brown and white feathers.

I have long, powerful claws.

I love to eat fish.

My sharp **beak** helps me rip up my food.

I live in a really large nest.

I was fuzzy when I was a chick.

Do you know what I am?

I'm a
Bald Eagle!

About Bald Eagles

1. Bald eagles' heads are covered in white feathers.

2. Bald eagles usually lay two eggs.

3. Bald eagles have long claws that they use to catch their **prey**.

4. A bald eagle weighs about the same as a house cat.

5. Bald eagles' favorite food is fish.

Glossary

chick (chik) a very young bird

fuzzy (FUHZ-ee) covered in fuzz

nest (nest) a home built by birds and other animals

powerful (POW-ur-fuhl) having great power, strength, or authority

prey (pray) an animal that is hunted by another animal for food

Index